THE MELODY OF LIGHT

Kalu Onwuka

Granada Publishing

Los Angeles, California

The Melody of Light

Copyright 2014 © Kalu Onwuka

Published in Los Angeles, California by Granada Publishers. Granada Publishers is wholly owned by Granada Publishing Company, Los Angeles, California.

Granada Publishing titles may be purchased in bulk for educational, business, fundraising or sales promotional use. For information please e-mail **sales@granadapublishing.com**.

All rights reserved. No part of this publication may be reproduced, stored in a retrieval system, or transmitted in any form or by any means-electronic, mechanical, digital, photocopy, recording or any other-except for brief quotations in printed reviews, without the written permission of the copyright owner.

Library of Congress Cataloging-in-Publication data.

The Melody of Light/Kalu Onwuka

LCCN: 2014932730

ISBN: 978-0-9900203-9-4

ISBN: 0990020398

Printed in the United States

Dedication

I will like to dedicate this book *The Melody of Light*, which is part of *Poems in Faithfulness to the Divine* series, to all those who have shared the gifts of light and love with me either in formal or informal settings. You are too numerous to count but you have my heart-felt gratitude. I will also like to share the series with all those who love poetry and the everlasting beauty of simple words fitly spoken. Oftentimes in life, the will to act is not so much enabled in what is said but how it is said.

Acknowledgments

As always, I will first like to acknowledge Christ Jesus as the Lord of my life. He is my muse and it is his Spirit that enables me to write. Also, I will like to acknowledge that it is not possible to see through an undertaking such as *Poems in Faithfulness to the Divine* series without the loyal support of family, friends and well-wishers. You have all been there from the conception, writing and the publication process. I will like to acknowledge all your help for you continue to give me cause to hope for the best in mankind. It is such goodness that you share that evokes the pure love and good hope for better extolled within these poems.

CONTENTS

Dedication	iii
Acknowledgements	iv
Foreword	xii
In Divine Thrust	1
Able to Reach Heaven	3
Humility's Passageway	5
Sweet Spot Above	7
The True Wealth	10
Plea for Mercy	11
A Recycling Project	13
Kindness of Destiny	15
Forever Divine	17
Lost Wings Found	19
Hand of Faithfulness	20
A Sad Tale	22

CONTENTS

Chiseled in Love	23
Common Thread	25
Reborn into Immortality	27
Deep Nail Marks	29
The Citizen	31
Truth in Pictures	33
Love Reconnected	35
Trail Blazers	37
Glory of the Cross	39
The Sublime	41
Golden Flakes of Mercy	43
Embodiment of Truth	45
Branch of the Tree	47
The Entombed	49
Breaking the Chains	51

CONTENTS

Ode to the Divine	53
By the Divine Dove	55
Saga of Eternity	58
The Good Thing	60
Candle Lights of the Divine	62
Exalted in Love	64
The Good and Evil	67
Cloak of Wisdom	70
Ascendant Spirit	72
Wisdom of Love	74
Light against Darkness	75
Language of Truth	78
Realm of Fulfillment	79
Together from Time	81
Learn to Listen	83

CONTENTS

Melody of Life	85
The Simple life	87
Confused and Faithless	89
Harmony thru Peace	91
The Plain and Secret	93
Wonder of Rebirth	95
Urge to Perfection	97
Buyer Beware	99
Matured in Faith	101
The Backpack	103
The Grand and Little	105
Sharing the True	107
The Blessed man	109
An Intimate Means	111
For Circumcised Hearts	113

CONTENTS

Fulfillment in Godliness	115
Rain Man	117
Immunized in Goodness	120
In Safety of the Ark	122
A Way Home	124
Search for Better	126
The Utility Vehicle	128
Ode to the Samaritan	130
Ride the Wind	132
The Ill-Suited Companion	134
The Well Digger	137
In Quietness	139
Weeds of Life	141
The Fit Gardener	142
Son of the Father	144

CONTENTS

The Perfect Gift	146
Mercy seeks in Hope	148
The Matured Tree	150
The Poor that Inherits	152
Soul of the Swine	154
A Song in the Heart	156
Pictures Within	158
Paradise on Earth	160
False and Compromised	162
Cogs in the Divine Wheel	164
Triumphant in Life	167
Changes thru Drought	169
Earthly and Cosmic Clocks	172
Fusion than Fission	174
From Land of Truth	177

CONTENTS

Power in Words	179
Treasure the Soul	181
Mirror of Indictment	183
Heart of the True Confessor	185
Higher and Greater	188
The Climb	190
Bond of Love	192
Little Folly	194
Seed of Bitterness	196
Morning Appointed for Truth	198
From Same Womb	200
Good and Lovely	202

FOREWORD

This book titled *The Melody of Light* features selected works of poetry from four previous works that include *Anthems in the Glorious Dawn, In Enchantment of Eternity, Tones of the Stellar* and *A Splendid Awakening*.

Consisting of roughly one hundred different poems, *The Melody of Light*, tackles varying subjects that nevertheless unite through a thread consisting of love, truth and light. With simplicity and beauty, these poems demonstrate how the power of true enlightenment can protect man against the wickedness that pervades our everyday lives as well as help foster a deeper spiritual understanding through clever poetical devices. With words that capture man's eternal journey toward a connection with a divine higher power, the verses contain subtle themes of hope, redemption, and love that are sure to inspire all readers.

With each verse painting vivid images of the power that enlightenment can bring, *The Melody of Light* highlights the fact that the divine way is man's only sure defense against the vagaries of a capricious world. Brimming with valuable insight and thoughtful lessons, these poems represent different facets of the eternal human quest for a meaningful relationship with God and all around him.

Kalu Onwuka

In Divine Thrust

Much can be transformed in a fleeting moment

By thunder and lightning borne of a common thrust

Incredible burst of energy it takes to lift the curtain

And rend heaven's veil for a glimpse into the hidden

It takes that dreaded by fearful and ignorant minds

By blind masses gripped in the throes of uncertainty

To bring gift of enlightenment to those who seek

Such minds inspired by truth that aspire to know

The illumination received in the streak of lightning

Much like the inspiration that visits man in a flash

Is a potent sign in the heavens to tell the seeker

That all things can be known in the light of Truth

In Divine Thrust (Cont'd)

Thunder and lightning may seem like dissimilar pairs

But are complementary twins from divine's breath

As hammer strikes the anvil and sparks fly to say

All things wrought on earth are first forged above

Lightning streaks to offer a heavenly perspective

In brief flashes to offer enlightenment in darkness

Tis torch needed to clear man's cluttered mindscape

A light given to induce vision and rekindle purpose

The flame of wisdom is a gift that can only dwell

In minds rid of fear and doubt that love the truth

In feet lighted to take timely and orderly steps

With outstretched hands that receive with thanks

End

Able to Reach Heaven

Sons of Providence; Daughters of Zion

Are all connected as offspring of Light

Into the realm of infinite possibilities

The limitless which never stops giving

Beyond the horizon into timelessness

To become transformed into the being

With soul of the eagle in body of a man

Befits the one for all seasons and ages

The faithful well-fitted is the righteous

A man with a spirit that'll abide forever

For he has become the golden-hearted

In the ever trusting love of the Divine

Able to Reach Heaven (Cont'd)

He is one who has received the precious

For faith has rewarded him with the way

Taken away at Babel a long time ago

The means to reach Heaven from earth

End

Humility's Way

An Impending doom looms not too far
As a comb now sorts through humanity
Tis hand of God that holds sway there
Knows who to keep and what to discard

To live in fullness of light is the reprieve
Calls for love of truth and sincere belief
For life governed by the words of truth
Will find refuge and escape into new life

There's a ladder that leads into freedom
From darkness below into light above
Tis same escape lifted Jacob into Israel
Leads from the earthly to the heavenly

Humility's Way (Cont'd)

Not by the works of the flesh or mind

But in the spirit of love through light

Given to those who yield to divine's will

And seek after God in sincere humility

Humility's passage is that rare gift of life

That is seen with eyes of faith not sight

The precious received by grace thru faith

Is for him who walks in true light to find

End

Sweet Spot Above

A special place where noble spirits dwell
Is spiritual realm that is far above the world
Place for men and angels to be neighbors
Where mortals become privy to Divine's will

Top of God's mountain; heaven's tableland
Is the place for the chosen to find true rest
Just like the communication satellites above
In a sweet spot between heaven and earth

By trusting God the faithful do come to find
Sense of true self and their place in creation
Where all's in harmony and there is nothing
To perturb the universal order and scheme

Sweet Spot Above (Cont'd)

Sweet spot above is the place of the sacred

Where the veiled and eternal are to be known

Measured words of truth from beyond man

There to be entrusted to only noble souls

Man becomes means by which divine wisdom

Priceless and precious may be shared by all

Not for the profane to use for selfish ends

But for the worthy to use for mankind's aid

End

The True Wealth

The events glimpsed from behind the curtain of time
Are sprinklings of golden dust showered from above
As the rare and priceless to be safeguarded at all costs
For therein is essence of the everlasting and enduring

The precious which the faithful seek populate Heaven
As the substance of life and power that makes old new
All by divine wisdom and knowledge revealed to man
For the purpose of redemption and rebirth in spirit

The faithful pilgrim suffers temporary loss in the world
To become the noble in spirit laden with much wealth
Such that is availed is not the kind found in the world
But the needful and fulfilling that afford true peace

The True Wealth (Cont'd)

The man that serves in the way that true love demands
Where one life is laid down so that many will abound
His offspring will bathe in the blessings of the Creator
For the promises and blossoms of love belong to them

Such a householder who serves in faith and compassion
Has a tabernacle to enlarge and greater flock to receive
He's bestowed with much for work done in faithfulness
Good gifts that neither thieves nor robbers can touch

Man's true wealth is children both natural and spiritual
God fearing fruits borne of the tree of righteousness
As the means to measure humanity's bloom or blight
To crown life's work and uphold man in his old age

End

Plea for Mercy

The way of light affords man the better choice

As passage way of humility to lead to the exalted

Tis an upward way for man to escape the earthen

And to have good fruits of peace and the eternal

Most of humanity have rejected the way of light

But chosen the downward thrust into the earthen

Where a gloomy doom and traumatic end awaits

In a future needlessly sacrificed for lusts and wants

The world's not meant to be man's final destination

Only a spaceport for those with the passport of Life

Launch-pad from where the noble in spirit ascend

To an exalted and better home in heavenly places

Plea for Mercy (Cont'd)

Man will always be like a worm that crawls in dust
And never make the get-away to his home above
As long as he is determined to seek by his flesh
For passage from earth to heaven is found in spirit

Tis pointless for man to wrestle with the divine
For he cannot ascend by his wits and own terms
He'll scheme as Jacob and never 'see' in that way
For only by plea for mercy will Israel seek and find

End

A Recycling Project

There's life in the kingdom of light availed to some
Many know not that life and have missed the Truth
Such are those that seek to sit pretty on earth
Men at great risk of condemnation and damnation

Such often seek and find fool's gold to heart's fill
Blind men who cannot see that the earth is a dump
Constantly being recycled by a non-wasting mind
Who searches with care to save the redeemable

Sooner or later the point of no return is reached
When the good are salvaged and the job is done
Nothing worth redeeming left but pure garbage
Trash to be burned so the pristine can duly emerge

A Recycling Project (Cont'd)

The regeneration of the earth is by order of heaven

And begins with the faithful redeemed for new life

Such are the founding seedlings for the advent age

Worthy ones recycled into an everlasting kingdom

End

Kindness of Destiny

The messenger of light is that Holy Cow
Reared to maturity in barnyard of God
The sacred who exists not for the flesh
But for meat of the spirit borne in mercy

The matured in spirit is a soul at peace
Who's merged into unity with the Divine
To escape death and become timeless
A universal spirit who lives for all ages

The heavenly Father's lot is his business
And the kindness of destiny his blessing
For him who let go of fame and fortune
Saw those impostors for what they are

Kindness of Destiny (Cont'd)

Fame and fortune are rewards at best
To be blessed is far better and timeless
For blessings come not with misgivings
But are good everywhere and anytime

Eternal life under goodness and mercy
Is availed thru the kindness of destiny
As the package that includes all things
So the heart's desires are ever fulfilled

End

Forever Divine

When truth and light lead man
Into the love that never gives up
Life is glorified beyond measure
So that death's grip is loosened

True glory belongs to the Creator
And things do become glorified
When God plays a decisive role
In the earthly endeavors of man

Eternity becomes the destination
When man's footstep is after God
He'll come into realm of delights
To join love's everlasting songfest

Forever Divine (Cont'd)

Eternity is for the forever divine

For man of faith deemed worthy

To receive the precious gift of Life

And cease from the fear of death

Then is death no longer a sad end

But the start of a great journey

As continuation in a forever-land

Of a glorious life in new awakening

End

Lost Wings Found

Man loses his spiritual wings upon exit from the womb

Loses it as he views the world with the eyes of the flesh

To be soon left as time passes with nothing but the ego

As a spiritually moribund entity that craves earthly glory

The man of flesh can be transformed in the light of truth

So a new self emerges after due spiritual transformation

Reborn to re-discover his wings and use them to soar

As a higher breed to alternate 'tween heaven and earth

The reborn is no longer a mud crawler bound to earth

But a gentleman whose mind is able to touch heaven

And rub off as desired from the lamp of divine genius

So an earthling can begin to see in light of the heavenly

End

Hand of Faithfulness

The reborn spirit is the reward and result

With the good and perfect also received

By souls that feed and live on God's truth

Who seek after life's enduring and fulfilling

Sad is the empty soul that rejects the truth

For the divine gifts are not availed to him

Discontentment is all that is left in his life

For such who have no reverence for Light

With the right hand man reaches out to God

To receive with humility and thankful joy

But with the left hand he touches the world

To give and share with all in comradeship

Hand of Faithfulness (Cont'd)

Right hand of the faithless withers in time

For without faith man is a stranger to God

Who's not able to receive that which endures

For he lacks the means to reach the divine

Takes right hand to put up resistance to evil

And hold up the shield of faith for protection

In a world full of wickedness and evil deeds

Where acts of men differ from what they say

End

A Sad Tale

The man famished in soul is discontent within

A tale of dearth from spiritual estrangement

He hungers for things that bring no fulfillment

With desires that serve as fuel for raging fires

A malaise that defines many lives on earth

Leads in a downward spiral to the bottomless

To live in unceasing hunger and consumption

As maggots that writhe with insatiable crave

Man trapped in a cycle of wants and purges

Is the fool led away into the barren lands

Empty places where there is no living water

With no way of escape save by light of truth

End

Chiseled in Love

To be rewarded with despise and mockery

And be condemned for the guilt of others

Is the worst that man can do to another

For choosing divine's way of love and hope

Man of good deeds rejected by the world

Through his heavy cross soon does come

Into a place reserved around Divine's table

To experience fullness of the riches of God

The innocent who suffers on account of love

With grace that never makes a complaint

Soon enters into a covenant with the Divine

To receive the best that Heaven offers man

Chiseled in Love (Cont'd)

Such is the faithful remade in the Father's image

One to be well attended by goodness and mercy

For love that's proven to be true and unfeigned

And for faith demonstrated beyond all measure

Blessings of the Father do follow him always

The beloved and chosen one who dwells secure

Within the cleft hewn in the rock of all ages

With the hammer of faith and chisel of love

End

Common Thread

The faithful is able to see the common thread
The harmony and overall truth in scriptures
That binds the sacred words into one whole
And speaks about a paradise lost to mankind

It resounds with pleas of the Father's anguish
As he waits for the lost children to come home
In pained love that aches with a longing desire
For the creature to bond again with his Creator

It decries the path and pitfalls of transgression
Through prideful disobedience and sinful ways
In sadness for the fruit fallen far from the tree
But with hope always for timely reconciliation

Common Thread (Cont'd)

In words that laud love's long suffering nature

With the readiness to forgive all and to forget

Such frame an offer of peace and redemption

So man can know self and find true purpose

In the reconciliation and peace with the Father

Man finds that sought and hoped for since Eden

A place of honor reserved and ready welcome

At the Creator's communal feast of love at last

End

Reborn into Immortality

New life awakened by spiritual conception

Is hatched in a cocoon of the Father's love

So man is reborn in the divine image in light

Able to receive the better that's truly sweet

To walk humbly and sincerely before God

In true confession and abstinence from sin

With the divine truths to guide man's steps

Is the all-important decision to make in life

The Father does forgive mankind thru love

When the heart is contrite and repentant

Sets such aside for a life of useful service

So redemption's song can ever resound

Reborn into Immortality (Cont'd)

Some he saves to be woven 'to fabric of life

As sons of light cloaked and duly suited up

With the fleece of the lamb well-sacrificed

That protects mortals from ravages of time

Life is to don immortality's seamless robe

Woven by the Creator who is ever timeless

Tis to have the golden fleece much sought

And walk in the Spirit that vanquishes death

Robes are for his tabernacles among men

The beloved chosen to be his dwelling places

Such baptized in truth and in fire of the Spirit

Are suited up to join Life's everlasting flock

End

Deep Nail Marks

All who have borne faith's cross up the hill

Know the pain that sacrificial love exacts

In passion shared thru common experience

By all who long for goodness of the divine

The crucified are bearers of the nail marks

Whose lives are laid down for love of Truth

With deep wounds inflicted by the hateful

As badge of honor and crest of the divine

Takes the deep nails to keep the old buried

And same it takes to set man free into Life

For there's a special place reserved for such

Where crucifixion's nails have left marks

Deep Nail Marks (Cont'd)

The deep nails used to crucify the faithful

Are painful yet soothed by mercy's touch

Takes such pains to open up a wellspring

And make pure water of life to flow freely

In pain one suffers for many to be healed

As acceptable sacrifice deep in man's soul

To embrace such is to receive of life freely

So goodness and mercy can ever abound

End

The Citizen

From the darkness of the world into marvelous light
The old joins in spirit with the divine to produce a hybrid
Such is a higher breed that's streamlined and quickened
A creature reborn in spirit that is able to soar freely

Weighty things of the world are pruned from the reborn
With the needful left to replace the fluffy and wasteful
So man's spirit can be free to ascend to exalted realms
To converse in places where eternal spirits congregate

Through wisdom's veil to reach the light and starry
Is for man of faith who has reconciled with the Father
To become a citizen of the realm where peace reigns
With ability to read the writings that spell divine edicts

The Citizen (Cont'd)

Such must ask of the Father all that his heart desires

And be ever willing to do what the Creator asks of him

He need only buckle down for the never ending ride

In faith's carousel that turns tween heaven and earth

End

Truth in Pictures

The divine mind expressed through mortals
Is mystery and genius of words of scripture
Mostly figurative but yet true and fulfilling
With nary a word that is out of place or time

The fruit of the fig from the tree of life
Is for those with good and certain measure
Men full of understanding and true wisdom
Who are ever in communion with the Divine

Man's languages do discriminate and divide
To muddle communication among humanity
Tis borne of Babel to throw man for a loop
So that the earthen is not taken to heaven

Truth in Pictures (Cont'd)

The heavenly conversations unfold as images

In the light of truth borne of words of truth

Then is a picture truly worth a thousand words

In medium that is universal and tells no lies

End

Love Reconnected

Man's desire to reconnect with the divine
May cost the faithful his place in the world
Turns out to be a worthy sacrifice after all
In order to find welcome into realm of light

A confident glow surrounds the reconnected
To govern everything that he says and does
Tis the light of hope that attracts all seekers
Gift to be used in noble service of the Father

The heart lit aflame with power of the divine
Has an assurance borne of love reconnected
With no room left there for the spirit of fear
As the testament of life and reason for hope

Love Reconnected (Cont'd)

Spirit of power and sharp mind equips man

To serve him well when love is reconnected

So he'll know the necessary and do the right

Always with due and prescient knowledge

Face of the future is when all is done in love

As the time to redress and not to impress

To treasure the enduring and fulfilling always

In meekness that inherits the earth for good

End

The Trailblazers

A critical mass of men and women there is
All over the world that love the way of light
Such have walked in faithfulness and truth
To arrive at the place close to divine's heart

Men bestowed with the heavenly attributes
Thru an unending and everlasting dynamic
Are enlightened ones held in the divine palm
As one carefully holds the precious pearl

The stars of the night sky are their emblems
Gardeners that tend earthly lots with care
Each star occupies the plot ordained for it
Foreknown and predestinated from time

The Trailblazers (Cont'd)

Each is a trail-blazer to break new grounds

The starry used to show and lead the way

As vehicles to realize the new from the old

So divine light can have the full sway of day

End

Glory of the Cross

There's a seed of the divine buried within each man

Tis a spirit of goodness that waits and hopes in him

Becomes precious and of great value in due time

If the ego's dirt can be dislodged and washed away

Tis the reason for the dreaded passion and agony

For instituting the process symbolized by the cross

It's shame and humiliation are the perfect tools

To nail down man's flesh and bury the ego in dust

The cross is a divine platform for ascension of spirit

An icon of humiliation that serves as best teacher

For man to observe and learn clearly for all time

The mystery of spiritual purification thru humility

Glory of the Cross (Cont'd)

To understand the glory that the cross spawns
Is to marvel at the unfathomable wisdom of God
The ego denied of the praise it seeks soon vanishes
Into the nothingness of dust from which it came

The cross is an emblem of man's flesh rid of ego
Poised for takeoff to join the ranks of immortals
Tis there with his flesh yielded totally to the divine
That man is fitted with wings of an exalted spirit

It changes shameful death into a glorious victory
To afford the man without ego a new lease on life
So he can realize all that God has ordained for him
Who risked all that flesh can give in search of Life

End

The Sublime

Tis the desire of the righteous

That makes for things sublime

For man is such as he feeds

Be it in foolishness or wisdom

Within the figures of speech

That frame nuggets of truth

Are polishing hands of Love

To make the obedient shine

The veil of true understanding

Is lifted by the divine hand

Through faith's abiding love

For all who are willing to trust

The Sublime (Cont'd)

To receive in love from God
And abound in divine mercy
The sincere and humble know
To always ask in strong faith

The precious is like a pearl
A gift of long-suffering hope
Though not for those swine
Who deem grace for naught

Gift that comes to comfort
Is Holy Ghost from above
A sublime gift that comes
So man can know and have

End

Golden Flakes of Mercy

Mercy drops come down freely from above
As showers of latter rain to fill up the empty
Tis sweetness duly come in the season of hope
In fulfillment of love that's been saved for last

Gifts received in mercy are not to be wasted
Such are not for all but for the chosen faithful
For all who labor in love and in righteous works
Who are well watched with pride from above

From behind the veil mercy begins her journey
As golden flakes that descend to alight in love
On the righteous as divine showers that delight
For the heart that can see HIM hidden by light

Golden Flakes of Mercy (Cont'd)

The hand of Providence shows in timely order

As spirit takes flight while raptured in bliss

In such delightful moments that uplift the soul

With sweetness borne of mercy from above

End

Embodment of Truth

The noble in spirit is universal
Not bound by space and time
Can travel to far-away places
To realms beyond man's flesh

Faith makes an accommodation
For the truth alive in the heart
To spring forth to full life as due
When destiny's moment arrives

He never wanders far from truth
When man is anchored on faith
With good and certain purpose
In thoughts, words and actions

Embodiment of Truth (Cont'd)

As seasons and time converge

The words become the faithful

And man becomes the universal

As a living embodiment of truth

End

Branch of the Tree

Alas the hands of humble adoration

Have merged with wings of mercy

As the faithful is set free by truth

To soar into the realm of the eagle

Faithless that wanders from truth

Wings to bear him up will be clipped

He'll not rise with freedom's wind

But only know the dust of the lowly

He's salt that has lost its true savor

No longer good for anything in life

Not in God's way or in the world's

But only good as dirt of the earth

Branch of the Tree (Cont'd)

The soul well washed in living truth

Belongs with man reborn in light

Thru the certainty borne of eternity

As spirit readied for works of glory

He's one anointed in the divine vein

And issued the grand passport of life

Into a realm of the pure and true

As a branch of the righteous tree

Man's lot is with God and not men

To receive life's good and perfect

In requests and petitions granted

For the branch that withstands evil

End

The Entombed

The cleansing water of the living truth

That washes the heart of the faithful

Turns into joyful wine of marital bliss

As man's spirit joins up with the divine

Such that is joined dwells not in tombs

But has entered 'to eternity's freedom

Where much is availed to him as due

Far from the dead end of faithlessness

The future is veiled for tomb dwellers

As to look back is all that's left for such

Thoughts on things that might've been

About a past that should be forgotten

The Entombed (Cont'd)

Without vision man sacrifices the future

To become a blind follower of crowds

Who lacks the anointing and immunity

Availed by justification thru Godliness

End

Breaking the Chains

There! Is a man recreated in divine's image

When spirit mounts up with wings of eagle

With a heart that beats with compassion

And a mind re-connected with the Creator

An ordained and purposed life awaits him

Whose soul is washed and purified in truth

A place in congregation of the living is his

As one deemed worthy to serve the divine

Man has to stand tall so as to be trusted

With the gift that mercy affords in light

He's to overcome fears and venture afar

To where those perfected in love attend

Breaking the Chains (Cont'd)

The man appointed to step outside the box

And break the chain of human mediocrity

Must go beyond the gates of the known

For thereabouts is glory ordained for him

End

Ode to the Divine

You have brought me into marvelous light
The darkness and shadows have receded
You have given me a sunny snapshot of life
What I have long desired and yet will have
Yes, all that ail me are now fleeing

You have led me to the stream of living water
Where my parched soul will be refreshed
As I kneel down to drink with humble thanks
Pure water that flows from the divine throne
Yes, all that ail me are now fleeing

Ode to the Divine (Cont'd)

I have tarried with hope on the strait path

Seemingly alone but kept along through faith

You have led me to the Parkway of mercy

To cherish and amaze at what grace can avail

Yes, all that ailed me have now fled!

End

By the Divine Dove

Death and gravity claim no hold
In the heavenly and starry places
For perfection is at work up there
In, around and through all things

Perfection sought appears close
But remains far and out of reach
Yet it beckons the seeker ahead
Becomes urge for spread of light

No man is perfect but only God
The faithful do come close enough
Thru the divine perfecting process
Availed man thru the Holy Ghost

By the Divine Dove (Cont'd)

He speaks little but says so much

In whispers to the attentive heart

So that he can be duly informed

And have all that he should have

The sons do have due knowledge

The manna needed for daily living

In tweets and updates received

From the dove of the Holy Ghost

Sent from wisdom's source above

To avail the faithful peace within

Shows him the issues to attend to

And traps of the enemy to avoid

By the Divine Dove (Cont'd)

Such cannot be beguiled or misled

By contriving and conniving men

For tis not possible to deceive him

Man informed by the Holy Ghost

End

Saga of Eternity

To do the impossible and overcome the world
Into place of increasing dawn and the limitless
Is to receive the desired passport of eternal life
Into realm of boundless and infinite possibilities

Master is in the disciple as father is in the son
Disciple is in the master as the son in the father
Worthy disciple can do more than the master
Yet the son can never be above the father

The master takes the disciple into truth and light
The disciple takes the old master into the new
Tis true and undying love realized thru eternity
In the saga of lives awake in resurrection's dawn

Saga of Eternity (Cont'd)

Master dies but lives on in the worthy disciple
As sons and fathers who take endless walks
In a communal spirit within the halls of wisdom
As curators of humanity's collective goodness

The hushed voices of wisdom all blend together
Sages of the present and of ages gone before
Whispered truths that resound in noble hearts
In fleeting moments that dazzle as sunlight

The things that are pure do glow from within
To enlighten the way for all who seek after light
On eternity's trail paved with enduring truths
For hearts and minds filled with wisdom's love

End

The Good Thing

Narrow and winding is the trail
Path on which goodness strides
Broad enticing way of the world
Thereon evil masquerades as good

A caution to all that flock to buy
Beware of the world's promises
Her way is to sugarcoat all things
To beguile and delude the mind

Good is not the easy and sweet
But that which endures to fulfill
Good thing in life may be bitter
But the offspring is ever sweet

The Good Thing (Cont'd)

The good thing demands sacrifice

To initiate and then to maintain

Goodness is built on a foundation

Of truth, purpose and good care

Good thing that taxes man so much

Is not of vanity but of humble stock

Pays back profitably in its due time

Always fulfilling and ever enduring

End

Candle Lights of the Divine

The vaunted and revered scholarly systems

Gazes into shadows and reflections of light

But the sons of enlightenment are spawned

And woven together in living and loving light

Divine anointing is bestowed from above

Chosen not by intellect but by the heart

The sons have not gazed in its reflections

But have become immersed into pure light

Strong faith is found in truth, light and love

In the spiritual baptism of life's wilderness

Far from the presumptive and the limiting

Not through the conceited intellect of man

Candle Lights of the Divine (Cont'd)

To walk in under-appreciated love by many

With no ill-will to bear towards any man

Tis because the faithful are fully reassured

With the exalted love of the divine Father

Such anointed to serve the divine purposes

Are the ambassador spirits sent from above

Pollinating bees that help the promising

To become fruitful in the fullness of time

Men that lug the heavy cross in humility

As candle lights that withstand evil winds

Do bear good fruits ripe for divine harvest

For they draw others to the way of light

End

Exalted in Love

To walk in ancient trails of custodial spirits
Tempered with the blood of sacrificial love
Is to be forged in light's crucible of truth
And be purified in spirit from base to pure

The purified in spirit do keep in good care
Their vessels for honorable use by God
Truths that other men are precluded from
Are theirs to know and in fullness to have

They're primordial seeds of every new age
Sanctified to serve the cause of the divine
Good souls kept by the heavenly Father
Used to initiate the cause of regeneration

Exalted in Love (Cont'd)

Strangers in the world who are not of it
Woven from golden strands of the eternal
These rejected sojourners when embraced
Help many souls to find good purpose in life

These are men fit for the living congregation
Who are the vessels kept for greater honor
And held to a higher standard of judgment
Not as mere mortals but gods among men

He that is given the tools to do the amazing
Must honor the Father's call and bring forth
For him will be works that shine before men
To heaven's glory and to stellar distinction

Exalted in Love (Cont'd)

Tis a long great journey into regeneration
As the Father sheds his glory on the sons
In endearing rewards and enduring blessing
For the pleasure of both heaven and earth

Works commissioned for God last for life
Those for the praise of men only for awhile
Takes the good works to be exalted in love
And afford the wherewithal for eternal glory

End

The Good and Evil

The intoxicating beat of the world

Is a syncopation of good and evil

Tis the fruit of the forbidden tree

A little bite and be hooked for life

The good and evil are now mixed

Hard for man to tell them apart

Blind as a bat as he has become

In a world of glitz, buzz and fuzz

The masters of this world know

How to mask evil to look like good

They know that men go for looks

And charm them most thru the eyes

The Good and Evil (Cont'd)

The evil shepherds do lack in love

And make slaughter of the sheep

They beguile and mislead the flock

With false promises hard to deliver

Tis motive and intention of the heart

That determine what is good and evil

Good deeds must always be done

For the welfare and benefit of all

Unbridled lust for fame and fortune

Amid clamors for name recognition

Should never be motivation to act

For such make not for good works

The Good and the Evil (Cont'd)

Man's cravings and supersized ego

With its constant appetite to be fed

And his voracious desire to be praised

Has made goodness rare among men

End

Cloak of Wisdom

Wisdom found in age and experience
Can be entrusted to the worthy in spirit
Who has come into the realm of mercy
Even if he is young as men count age

The wise in spirit defies the limits of time
For he will be in covenant with the divine
The young in age who is faithful and true
Will be worthy to wear wisdom's cloak

He'll live in a place beyond man's flesh
And walk in the greater light of God
Where man's feet can never stumble
For space and time matter little there

Cloak of Wisdom (Cont'd)

Wisdom that wears the cloak of youth

Has untied the leash that constrains man

Where the truth has made the spirit free

There! Is a living billboard for divine glory

End

Ascendant Spirit

The ascendant spirit has set the flesh at naught

To be welcomed into the divine fold as a son

Belongs nowhere but yet belongs everywhere

Belongs with no one but belongs with all men

Lives for all yet makes no demand on anyone

He loves all men but he loves God above else

His footsteps of love are the seed pods of life

This child of love walks on earth without fear

For he thinks, speaks, acts and serves all in love

To make the dying things find new life again

Ascendant Spirit (Cont'd)

Ascendant spirit that has overcome the world

Man that soars on the glorious wings of faith

Through the uplifting stream of the divine wind

Will not bed down in the heart of the earth

For his heart has found the heavenly home

End

Wisdom of Love

Life triumphant that snatches victory from death

Spawns countless offspring from the womb of life

Wherever the divine impulse governs man's will

In wisdom of love blended and distilled in time

Tis due wisdom that sets the imposing at naught

Insightful knowledge that speaks to the mountain

To move it out of the path of truth and light

So men can see and declare the goodness of God

It only asks the mind to be set on the things above

That men love each other as they love themselves

To uphold and live in the spirit of justice for all

So benevolence and kindness be not cast aside

End

Light against Darkness

To be safe from damages and ravages

Things that destroy most men in life

And be at ease with peace in the heart

Is man's lot when he's reborn in Light

Locked in bitter and life long battle

Ordained from the foundation of time

Light and darkness can find no accord

Always has been and will ever continue

Light brings on life and dons a smile

Nature cannot wait to embrace its rays

Light calls all to join in songfest of love

An ode to creation and all that's good

Light against Darkness (Cont'd)

Darkness loves death and wears a frown

To hold nature in an apprehensive grip

Dons the mask of fear that douses hope

Aims to kill dreams of Creation's spawn

There's a wall in place to sort things out

Firmament of hope to save from death

Shield that separates light and darkness

With passage only by divine anointing

Quite a firm membrane of separation

That keeps life from the touch of death

Tis smaller than the eye of the needle

Yet quite easy for a camel to pass thru

Light against Darkness (Cont'd)

A sacrifice to make and a price to pay

For passage from darkness into the light

The wise man does sell all that he has

So he can pass from death on to Life

End

Language of Truth

Universal language of truth
Simple as there ever was one
The language of this or that
Yes or no and dos or don'ts

Tis the language of the heart
Heard by the purified in truth
The upright and firm in spirit
Marked to hear the inaudible

Tis borne of the Holy Ghost
Tweets received in real time
To assure the sons of Heaven
The Holy Spirit is near to help

End

Realm of Fulfillment

The realm of eternal life can be known

With eye of the spirit that sees in Light

Tis a garden of trees laden with fruits

Where the Father communes with sons

Garden where immortals take a walk

Amid knowledge and tools of creation

Where true fulfillment can be found

For joy and peace is there to be had

Tis fulfillment found at meeting point

Where heaven and earth kiss in love

For thereabouts in sweetest concord

Wisdom whispers man's purpose to him

Realm of Fulfillment (Cont'd)

Takes wisdom to endure in the way

On the long and winding walk of faith

Same calls the faithful into communion

So the creature can know his Creator

End

Together From Time

The heart of the faithful in love
Is washed in pure light of truth
To come into that understanding
Which hungers after the divine

The impurities of an evil world
Keep many separated from God
Only when the soul is cleansed
Can man know the greatest love

Love is the force which wakes up
The dormant spirit asleep in man
To seek return to the abode of Life
Source from where all came to be

Together from Time (Cont'd)

Those who come home to Love

Are all spawns of a common womb

Kindred folk knit together from fore

As one from the foundation of time

End

Learn to listen

In the weakest moments

So clear and so certain

A voice of hope comes

To calm troubled hearts

In the hopeless times

And the darkest hours

Then in boundless love

Tender mercies alight

The dark seasons repeat

As night follows the day

Only to let man know

He is little before God

Learn to Listen (Cont'd)

In down moments of life

Is when hope is reborn

As man learns to trust

Life and love reappear

Tis help in nick of time

Voice that tutors in hope

Still, calm and reassuring

That says never give up

Takes truth in the heart

To keep dimness away

For with light in the soul

All thoughts come to life

End

Melody of Life

Sun always shines for all

With glee upon its face

Ever in joyful exuberance

With no sad tales to tell

The sweet melody of life

Plays the enchanting tunes

In dawn of each morning

As birds awake to tweet

Do not forget the flower

That cannot wait to unfold

In colors and sweet nectar

To say life is good indeed

Melody of Life (Cont'd)

Sun's always eager to hear

A refrain of life's melodies

With flame of love in heart

Nothing can douse the 'sol'

End

The Simple Life

Needless things clutter man's life

With no room for good to abound

A deadly grip that chokes the spirit

So sickness and death can parade

The simple life in orderly living

Puts focus on the things above

With little of it on things below

So fulfillment can have the day

The true self that is at his core

Man can find by pruning his life

The part that responds to truth

Knows there's no shame in light

The Simple Life (Cont'd)

With clarity afforded by true light

Not in conformity with the world

From the edge of life's wilderness

The man reborn can do all things

End

Confused and Faithless

The unclean feasts in the heart

Of the unworthy untrue to faith

That professes loudly before all

Just for show in false confession

He picks and chooses to suit

What to obey and when to do

One ruled by the spirit of caprice

With eyes for the praise of men

Good one day but not the next

With troubles that rift the soul

Deeply conflicted and torn apart

In the domain of the unstable

Confused and Faithless (Cont'd)

A bipolar existence is for him

The confused and faithless soul

Who neglects the steady rock

And builds on the shifting sand

End

Harmony through Peace

All things do talk to the other

When harmony is found in life

For there is a creative order

That underlies all the universe

Tis the consciousness of life

That speaks in one voice to all

To tear down veil of darkness

So the dead can wake in light

There is an ear in the heart

That lives to please the Father

Such is in tune with the divine

And will not stumble in life

Harmony through Peace (Cont'd)

To live in certain peace within

Is to room above in the spirit

So storms of life can become

Mere ripples that pass away

Peace that dwells in the heart

Is platform on which to stand

And receive with thankful joy

The enduring gifts from above

Peace within anchors the soul

Holds the key to fortune's door

Man that has no peace within

Has his portion with confusion

End

The Plain and the Secret

Praise and thanksgiving to the Father
Yield much from store of Providence
In knowledge and wisdom that shines
From Illumination's womb way beyond

The divine storehouse is readily opened
To grant the desires of faithful hearts
The plain and the secret to behold
Things hidden from foundation of time

In special offerings from Benevolence
As he shows his magnanimous hands
To faith wrought thru willing obedience
By the love that never fails to bless

The Plain and the Secret (Cont'd)

How wondrous divine goodness can be

As wisdom's apples turn to silver pictures

In gifts of the Father to his beloved sons

For whom he reserves the best in mercy

End

Wonder of Rebirth

Hourglass and figure eight

Iconic emblems of rebirth

As one half fills up the other

To begin the count anew

Matter soon changes face

And energy changes form

Hushed silence everywhere

At the wonder of rebirth

Alas the debased is purified

So the exalted can emerge

Amid bubbles of hopeful joy

As new is displayed in dawn

Wonder of Rebirth (Cont'd)

Under God's divine sunshine

Everything does get better

From the less to the greater

In the full passage of time

End

Urge to Perfection

Elder and young in faith
Form an irrepressible duo
That urges on the spread
Of truth and light in love

Each bears up the other
As all share in strength
Each to his fellow in love
So no one is left without

Tis recipe for the perfect
When the imperfect things
Are well blended in love
With a pinch of divine salt

Urge to Perfection (Cont'd)

The search for the perfect

Always seems to be near

Yet remains out of reach

To urge on spread of light

Wisdom of the highest

Does make things better

To turn human weaklings

Into pillars strong and fit

Tis an eternal sunshine

When hearts join as one

As flames fused thru love

In a reach for perfection

End

Buyer Beware

Wisdom that speaks to the heart

Does not change in tone or tune

But spirit that beguiles the flesh

Changes pitch to suit the sale

Offers man this but sells him that

Promises fulfillment to one and all

In deceitful ploys that delude many

And amount to weariness of flesh

In floods that deluge man's mind

With more than he can manage

Always besieging him with wants

In one flawed choice after another

Buyer Beware (Cont'd)

If this does not suit man's fancy

Then the other will be the candy

If the sour does not suit the palate

Then the sweeter will cut the cake

Counsel for vainglorious appetites

Let the unwary buyer be aware

Promises to deliver much for little

Always end up as good for nothing

End

Matured in Faith

The milk is for the young

Just starting on the way

He has no teeth to grind

Digest the meat of truth

Season comes in the life

Of the young in the way

Maturity calls out to say

Time to become a man

The time will never come

Unless the young is suited

To tune out and turn off

Foolish impulses of youth

Matured in Faith (Cont'd)

Tis then the roots of faith

Find anchor on solid rock

So the child can step up

To be chiseled into a man

End

The Backpack

An oversized backpack in life

Will weigh heavily on man

Smaller one with the needed

Helps to ease life's burdens

Good choices along the way

That pare down the baggage

Lightens man's load in life

To spare him troubles ahead

An easy yoke in life does well

Helps man be worthy in light

So his spirit is always tuned

To hear the still voice of hope

The Backpack (Cont'd)

Hope makes worthy sacrifices

As seeds of goodness sown

Soon to be harvested in time

As blessings that abound in life

End

The Grand and Little

From a divine impulse all things came

Man must never be deluded otherwise

An all-knowing wisdom did create it all

The son that knows can create as well

As the father does good sons can too

Like cookies baked in the same mold

The colors vary but the process is same

Takes time, water, heat and pressure

Same mind and motif diligently at work

The same yesterday, today and forever

Sons remade in the image of the Father

To remake earth in the order of heaven

The Grand and Little (Cont'd)

'Little' heavens being created on earth

With divine aesthetics still in command

In the grand as well as in the little plot

Only difference being in scale and size

The divine motivation never changes

Transformation in soul, mind and body

To serve and give man foretaste of glory

And afford him very good days on earth

To him bestowed with the divine mind

Will be sublime and blissful moments

It's all there waiting for man to have

Thru the anointing of the Father on sons

End

Sharing the True

Rendezvous with the divine

Is not in buildings or groups

Only on the long lonely walk

And that is the gospel truth

The bond with the divine

For those who seek to know

And are willing to be told

Takes place by one on one

To share the truth is hard

It falls mostly on deaf ears

Those with the will to share

Are certain and strong in love

Sharing the True (Cont'd)

For his works to be sublime

And shine before men's eyes

The faithful must play a part

To help Love's light shine thru

End

The Blessed Man

The misinformed man believes

But it is quite far from the truth

That material prosperity is proof

A man's way is pleasing to God

Tis welcome when goods abound

If not tainted by lust and greed

Rewards exist and also blessings

A big difference between the two

Reward is okay but much limited

A blessing is a far different matter

In multiple ways and many areas

A blessing is a gift that never ends

The Blessed Man (Cont'd)

Only the blessed man is attended

By rare gifts of goodness and mercy

As window of heaven's never closed

For the faithful man truly blessed

A blessing is that binding covenant

True and faithful companion in life

Tis not bound by season or place

Ever there when hearts beat for God

End

An Intimate Means

There is an intimate means

By one loving heart to another

The father uses to commune

With the faithful in the way

Means for the father to fold

Loving arms around his own

He's the Holy Ghost from above

That only the Father can send

Tis for those with ear to hear

In the gesture that speaks to say

I am now with you through life

Never to leave or abandon you

An Intimate Means (Cont'd)

A sure affirmation for those

Exalted from grace unto mercy

Given to comfort and show man

A grand way to a higher plane

The higher is Heaven's tableland

A place to join the conversation

What more is there to seek for

Than to be privy to mind of God

End

For Circumcised Hearts

Heed the man within pleads a voice
Inaudible yet quite clear as crystal
Language sought after since Babel
That speaks deep from man's heart

Dare to look within it pleads with all
Let no darkness be found therein
Save truth and light locked tightly
In the sweet embrace called love

Language of heaven that says it all
Is for circumcised hearts to know
Such that the deaf can hear clearly
In warmth that the blind can feel

For Circumcised Hearts (Cont'd)

Tis called sweet language of Love

Let its healing essence flow freely

So that men's hearts can be tuned

To hear Life's soothing melodies

End

Fulfillment in Godliness

The entry way is a channel of light
That leads man to Love and into Life
For him to seek by any other means
Is to invite futility to be life's harvest

Disappointments do attend the way
When man trusts not to live by faith
Material goods is best he can gain
But to his surprise that won't suffice

Hunger he craves in the place within
The inner longing that haunts him so
Deep within the depths of his soul
Can be satisfied when spirit wakes

Fulfillment in Godliness (Cont'd)

To seek fulfillment and consolation

Through possessions and acquisitions

Is a quick way to bankrupt the soul

And be left with fool's gold at best

Tis the guiding light of the North Star

That leads to certainty and fulfillment

Only emptiness and wantonness is left

When man wanders far from its truth

End

Rain Man

Takes wings of the eagle to mount up

And be bestowed with a grander vision

In light that comes from meat of truth

To crown the faithful with divine wisdom

To see clear pictures within life's scripts

From the perch of the exalted heights

Is to stumble no more under the veiled

But to know in fullness in all that matters

The earthy spirits dwell in lowly places

And lack the wings that lift up the noble

Such that cannot soar to receive the pure

Are left to traverse beaten tracks below

Rain Man (Cont'd)

The low clouds of the sweet and easy
Are vapors of hot air that bear no rain
And fade away under scrutiny of light
To be dispersed by the winds of the times

The rain clouds are only found up high
In a starry realm where the eagles soar
Tis pure water that sustains true living
So life and goodness may abound in full

Up in the mountain pervaded with life
For only the pure of heart to ascend
There the cleansed in truth are baptized
With the essence of life's everlasting

Rain Man (Cont'd)

The baptized is called by the divine Spirit

To be a rain man who bears living water

As destiny demands and love urges him

Within Life's unending dance of eternity

End

Immunized in Goodness

The man in covenant with the divine
Travels in light to the heavenly places
He's an elect thru whom grace flows
In goodness and mercy to the lacking

Man that lives to bear up the infirm
With no thanks or praise from many
But doubt and derision from most
Knows that time will honor his deeds

Humiliation and rejection will come
Also hurts and scorn many to count
But the innocent is well protected
For Benevolence is near him always

Immunized in Goodness (Cont'd)

Man that performs in noble service

Gets to live in immunity of goodness

For the past has been made powerless

And impotent to touch destiny's own

End

In Safety of the Ark

Father reveals so much in these times

To hearts and souls matured in faith

New vision to see thru darkened veils

In season for man to come 'to full light

Stars of heaven have filled up the night

As the divine's hand unfolds the banner

In a great unveiling of the sacred truths

For the honorable and readied in spirit

The stars of heaven are purified souls

Given knowledge of the hidden truths

Gift of spiritual insight to understand

The divine will for the benefit of man

In Safety of the Ark (Cont'd)

Sons of light in places over the world

To foretell and plead with all in love

So that the attentive and the willing

Can join them in safety of God's Ark

End

A Way Home

Spiritual flight is man's dream come true
Completion of the journey begun long ago
From the salty marshes to the grassy plains
And finally home to a place in the heavens

A journey that ends in triumphant escape
To the better long desired and hoped for
Source of the living water that sustains Life
That only a chosen few do manage to find

Found by those souls who are led in spirit
And guided by the hand of divine wisdom
Tis the precious found on road less travelled
Not on the broad way preferred by most

A Way Home (Cont'd)

Search for living water is mimicked in nature

By migratory herds that traverse the land

Creatures of unpurified souls that engage

In a fruitless and misguided search on earth

The way to the source of Life points upwards

Tis not found thru bravado, might or strength

But found by the humble and lowly in the way

Through sincerity, charity, peace and love

The faithful man deemed lowly by the world

Same is the one exalted by the divine Father

And shown the way to come home into Life

There to know himself and be known by all

End

Search for the Better

Man's true home is his heavenly future

Not in the irredeemable earthly past

The unpurified soul looks to the past

But the purified searches in the future

Heavenly home is the continuing city

The enduring that will never pass away

For all who desire and hope for better

Up in heaven is where the search ends

To search in the world is to be a victim

As the blind to never know true victory

Who exhausts his limited time on earth

In a search that never reveals the door

Search for the Better (Cont'd)

The blind wonder what life is all about

Man can only know if he comes into Life

Some thru wisdom have come to know

Masters in light who have found the key

End

The Utility Vehicle

The faithful who aspires for heaven's delights
Must have a to-do list written in his heart
Therein is where the divine Spirit searches
To choose such projects that merit blessing

A foretaste of regeneration is the blessing
As things become less taxing and expedient
So days of struggles, shortfalls and pratfalls
Are soon gone to be forgotten for good

The past with its salty tears of tribulation
Have accomplished the desired goal indeed
When man has been grafted into the divine
To do the marvelous in power of the spirit

The Utility Vehicle (Cont'd)

The vehicle of the past often disappoints
Breaks down and strands man on the way
Mires him in clay of disappointment valley
Never can take him to the top of victory hill

Man grafted to the divine is never stranded
For he's a utility vehicle good for all seasons
That's powered by sunshine of divine love
And retooled to be fit for all terrains of life

Such is the diligent gardener who will tend
The fruitful trees planted in his earthly lot
As a bee readied for the propagation of life
With honey to produce and glory to savor

End

Ode to the Samaritan

Tis the Samaritan who gets the truth

And ends up on the righteous path

Offers up thanks when others do not

And can perceive the true and real

Tis the Samaritan that is intimated

With the wisdom that God is a Spirit

To worship and be known in truth

In communion anywhere and time

Tis the Samaritan that is intimated

With the truth that God doesn't care

For ancestry, pedigree or cathedrals

But seeks after the hearts of men

Ode to the Samaritan (Cont'd)

Tis the Samaritan that does labor on

In the last days and in true charity

To share a true vision of the divine

And bring in the last harvests of souls

Tis the Samaritan who shows all men

That God lives in the heart that bleeds

When faith's robbed and left for dead

Stepped over by an uncaring world

The Samaritan that's little in the world

Is the one that finds intimacy with God

Tis he that becomes life's true treasure

A heart where God makes his home

End

Ride the wind

The Spirit is that uplifting divine wind
Chooses when to rise and way to go
Tis God's mind that initiates its courses
Governs and justifies all its actions too

Just like the electrical current at work
Powers and flows thru a chosen tool
The faithful is that piece of equipment
Re-conditioned for use by the Divine

Takes the flow and power of the Spirit
Thru man to accomplish good works
He that yields in faith is often lifted
To do the lovely that is of good report

Ride the Wind (Cont'd)

Such must hold out his wings of faith

And glide along in glorious liberty

In obedient trust as the spirit leads

So divine's power can be displayed

Tis wind that rises only with occasion

When a certain task needs to be done

Same calls the faithful to ride and soar

Until the task begun is well and done

End

The Ill-Suited Companion

God's chosen is given an earthly helper
A companion divinely ordained for him
He takes the lead and initiative in life
With his helper at dutiful command

There's a mission and purpose that calls
But the helper seems ill-suited for them
With obvious faults and imperfections
When seen with the eyes of the flesh

God searches with eyes of the spirit
Uses base things to confound the wise
Makes his wisdom and power available
To change the ill-suited into best-suited

The Ill-Suited Companion (Cont'd)

The imperfect with mismatched parts
Is good companion for the faithful man
With short comings come hidden assets
That'll suffice him regardless of defects

The Father foresees and figures all out
Always for the best interests of his own
He reveals vital attributes not too soon
Offers them up in due season as needed

God's favorite tool is the faithful man
The helper is a cover from the elements
To shelter him from the irritating bugs
So he can be focused on task at hand

The Ill-Suited Companion (Cont'd)

The faithful labor as companions in spirit

With no complaints but wisdom to seek

'bout ways to bring out the best from all

That Providence avails God's own in life

The horse appointed for God's anointed

To assist in the labors ordained for him

Needless to look at its mouth for it'll do

As its strength lies within and not without

End

The Well Digger

The faithful that is borne from love's womb
Is a water bearer for all times and seasons
To nourish and nurse that availed thru faith
In labors of love to secure man's future

He's a well digger who opens up a fountain
Who knows where to dig when others don't
He makes the call that wakes the dormant
And brings up the water so life can abound

He who digs the well must have a helper
A companion for life to help him on the way
A mate with the gift to draw out the water
And put the waterman's labors to good use

The Well-Digger (Cont'd)

The companion ties it all together for him

So that his labors will not be for naught

Knows to give living water to thirsty souls

On the errands that serve the Master's will

End

In Quietness

The life of meditative and blessed quietness
Seeks for time to be alone with the divine
For pestering and distractive noises drown
The still small voice that guides man in life

The noise of the world to him is disquieting
For the solitary traveler on the road to Life
Who travels not with the hordes of mankind
But in the company of spiritual messengers

He does and bears much in blessed quietness
As led by an innate and intimate divine urge
With Providence always at hand to bless
To meet his needs and help him win battles

In Quietness (Cont'd)

Such is host to much goodness buried within

That are duly revealed in the fullness of time

He's given to recover the forgotten and lost

As one that brings new things into full view

End

Weeds of Life

Takes a lot of pruning to untangle a man
From all the un-necessary weeds of life
Also patience and wisdom at hand to guide
Wean him from the worldly in little steps

Ugly weeds do clutter the mind's garden
And inhibit spiritual growth and perception
Tis unneeded foliage that's mostly for show
Bears no fruits and serves little purpose

Weed that chokes man is ungodly living
Due to unbelief and dislike for way of truth
Much craving for the material is the root
That has to be pulled so the good can thrive

End

The Fit Gardener

Man in possession of key of knowledge

Must guard that which he has received

For he's become a gardener-custodian

Of the precious seeds of the amazing

He's to use patience and due diligence

To cultivate and bring out rare things

Precious gifts from heaven to earth

All from seed thoughts divinely served

The custodian must learn to master

The call that wakes life up from sleep

And the entombed to spring forth free

To dance in the joyful return of hope

The Fit Gardener (Cont'd)

The gardener fit to tend the precious
Whether in labors as well as in pleasure
Is always in communion with the Divine
Ever bonded in meditation and prayers

Well-informed about the seeds to plant
Where to plant and how to tend them
He's one with peace within who knows
That good increase has been promised

End

Sons of the Father

He that stands in mercy can ask
And receive the gifts of the Divine
He need not go through another
To bare his soul and make a request

Goodness and mercy attend such
All who receive and share in grace
One to pour and another to receive
Tis foundation on which faith rests

As the teacher is in the student
So the father lives through the son
The student or son is just a vessel
Containment for the gifts of love

Sons of the Father (Cont'd)

The worthy vessel that does retain

All that has been charged into him

In true faithfulness to his mentor

Is son worthy to become a father

End

The Perfect Gift

The journey on the upward bound way
Makes life to be supreme over death
The father is the selfless sacrifice made
And son is the perfection realized thru it

The gift made to the self is imperfect
As it seeks to glorify the imperfect self
But the gift to others in selfless sacrifice
Is perfection realized by the imperfect

The blessings bestowed and received
From the divine has much value in it
Tis the perfect locked up safely in man
From the reach of thieves and robbers

The Perfect Gift (Cont'd)

The perfect abounds in the divine heart

For the purified in truth with love for all

Tis borne on the wings of compassion

To wherever life has overcome death

End

Mercy Seeks in Hope

The purified in truth is a son of Hope
Who can rise higher and do the greater
For Hope is a spacecraft that lifts man up
To do the stellar that twinkles before all

The son of Hope is crowned with wisdom
And filled with gifts too many to count
But the key to unlock that buried within
Is to ask, hope and then receive in mercy

Mercy asks but little from the receiver
Only that all should share and honor God
Love and serve the 'Giver' of good gifts
So the goodness of the rain never ceases

Mercy Seeks in Hope (Cont'd)

Mercy seeks in hope and rewards with life

For without it death roams about freely

Hope is sunshine that lightens the heart

And dew that waters thirsty souls as well

End

The Matured Tree

The righteous man is a matured tree

There is no difference between the two

God's eye rests upon him at all times

Bearer of good fruits in the due season

Hands that embrace the lightning thrust

And legs to stand thru life's stormy trials

Is for him that bears the light of truth

And leads men into the domain of Hope

Wielder of the sword who speaks in truth

Is a magnet to induce others on to Light

He hears and does all in true faithfulness

In power and goodness of God to man

The Matured Tree (Cont'd)

Voice of God speaks thru righteous trees

Whose leaves and fruits nourish humanity

To bring healing balm to those in mourning

And a glimpse of morning to grieving souls

End

The Poor that Inherits

To seek for divine anointing through faith
A man must bury himself as a seed in the soil
The shell of the seed decays into the ground
But from its core a seedling of hope emerges

In the fullness of time from seedling to a tree
To produce life sustaining fruits to nourish all
Tis mystery of rebirth into the exalted realm
As willing death of the old so new can ascend

The exalted new is the anointed and chosen
Models the way for all who sincerely seek
Such is the commission of all matured in love
To lead the willing back into the divine fold

The Poor that Inherits (Cont'd)

Man that buries himself for the love of God
Awakes in the new infused with divine essence
To commune in spirit with the heavenly Father
As mortal that has merged with immortality

To be groomed in a cocoon of light and love
Is new life regenerated in the cloak of divinity
As a nymph to be timely unveiled when due
While the old yields within an obscured self

Little one with the potential for greatness
Is bestowed with great wealth within him
For perfect gifts are reserved for such to have
'Poor' that has the earth for an inheritance

End

Soul of the Swine

The soul of the swine

Is not that of a man

Belongs with the fool

Who lives for himself

He settles for the gifts

Neglects to share too

He hoards all he can

But has no fulfillment

Precious things of life

Is never for the knave

Who presumes to know

And will never be filled

Soul of the Swine (Cont'd)

The belly might be full

Laden with possessions

But soul is not content

As man craves for more

A stranger to the divine

Never knows the sublime

With stagnation in spirit

No new horizon for him

Unfaithful who does not

Bless God with his best

Will not awake in spirit

In image of the Father

End

A Song in the Heart

Songs that swell in the thankful

In voices tuned to sing in grace

Will lift man on the wings of joy

Into love's sunshine and warmth

The true and humble adoration

That flows out of self-impulse

From the wellspring of the heart

Is testimony to divine goodness

Evoked with unsolicited candor

From a secure place in the heart

Exuberant expressions thru faith

All speak 'bout love known in light

A song in the Heart (Cont'd)

Ode to frame the efficacy of grace

And the forgiving nature of mercy

'bout the unfailing promises of love

Such that sustain the walk of faith

Times, faces and places may vary

Narrative and sentiments are same

About faithfulness and abiding love

Takes song in the heart to tell it all

End

Pictures Within

Many pictures within the scriptures
With many parts and elements within
Some portions are easily understood
But the mysteries are not so plain

The infallible truths can be known
By the obedient and matured in faith
As seeds of the divine well concealed
That spring to life only in due season

Righteous before God will be shown
The pictures hidden within scriptures
But wisdom of the all-knowing Divine
Remains a puzzle for presuming minds

Pictures Within (Cont'd)

The veiled truths cannot be surmised

Can only be known thru experience

For such are progressively revealed

When humble hearts seek in sincerity

Truth is known through faithfulness

Its validity in hindsight of experience

The scriptures are a jig-saw puzzle

To be known as keys are duly availed

End

Paradise on Earth

Man can change and transform a plot of land
To reflect order and harmony of the heavens
He can create a paradise in his earthly plot
To reflect that which exists and dwells in him

The same Spirit that created the universe
Moves in man to create a heaven on earth
As in the little within so in the big without
But all is from heaven in kindness to earth

Heaven on earth is a paradise for the Divine
To commune and walk in fellowship with man
All who come into the abode pleasing to God
Will sense his heavenly presence thereabouts

Paradise on Earth (Cont'd)

Such who come to seek in sincerity and hope

Will search out the good gifts concealed there

For all who hunger and desire in good faith

Are afforded the lovely therein in good order

End

False and Compromised

Hypocrite that has been denied same

Works to hinder men from receiving it

Key of knowledge that he truly covets

Precious gift that sets noble souls apart

Labels the pure as blundering heresy

So the young may not embrace Truth

And parades himself as an angel of light

While he aims to shield out the true

The search for truth and understanding

So man can know the will of his Creator

Ends only when God finds that heart

Large enough to receive his handprint

False and Compromised (Cont'd)

The hearts God touches are such that love

To aspire for truth and seek after wisdom

Whose footsteps are guided by true light

And care not for the false or compromised

End

Cogs in the Divine Wheel

The sons of Light do mount up as eagles
Borne on the steps of a cosmic escalator
As cogs in a divine wheel that ever turns
From heaven down to earth and up again

Such cut a parabolic arc over humanity
So men can be uplifted with them thru light
To the womb of love and realm of Life
Back home from whence they were sent

The sons are given to overcome the world
For goodness that uplifts is laden in them
Tis treasure of heaven as the telekinetic
To help man lift the heaviness of darkness

Cogs in the Divine Wheel (Cont'd)

Such are ground breakers come to rebuild

The broken and the wasted bereft of hope

Through greater love that counts no cost

By power of truth and light over darkness

Cogs that can thresh mountains in the way

Are the teeth of justice for the poor as well

Who sets the earthly table for many without

Just like Father prepares and sets for them

Tis wisdom that reaches all who ask in love

In insight and keys to bedeviling problems

To guard against the onslaught of the evil

And darkness that attempts to screen light

Cogs in the Divine Wheel (Cont'd)

The sooner that men come into light of truth

Is sooner that the shroud that drapes the land

Is lifted so love's flame can touch all in hope

And spring trapped souls from the deadly pit

End

Triumphant in Life

The spirit triumphant is bestowed on the anointed
Watchman with eye of the spirit focused above
Such is one divinely led to take the righteous path
There to obtain in mercy and share in love with all

Takes grace to make mountains become mole hills
For without it problems do seem insurmountable
Aids the faithful bestowed with a spirit triumphant
To find that pass even where the mountain is real

The triumphant has the withal to thrive in all times
For the table of goodness and mercy is set for him
As one destined to travel calmly on life's long road
With the face of Benevolence ever smiling on him

Triumphant in Life (Cont'd)

Entrusted to him is great vision and strong faith

The ladder up to the celestial such turn out to be

That soon uplifts the earthly into the heavenly

And afford him victories that are stellar to behold

Great courage and wisdom is availed through faith

So life's problems turn into a garden of promises

Laden with the seedlings of amazing opportunities

For the spirit that triumphs through all challenges

End

Changes thru Drought

Drought or deprivation is often ordained

To play a transforming role in a man's life

Tis through the times when he is in lack

That the light of reality helps him to see

The things that are truly important in life

So he can sort his earthly lot as he should

Unimportant things take up much room

To encumber the soul and choke the spirit

Only when such that hold back are let go

Sorted and buried as part of life's trash

Does the spirit in man spring to full life

So he can afford to have the truly fulfilling

Changes thru Drought (Cont'd)

Cessation of the rain does bring deprivation

To the faithless man as well as the faithful

Takes three years for the good to be rooted

And same for root of the ugly weed to die

But the faithful is not much for wear thru all

For his needs are handy and are easily met

The faithful handles deprivation well enough

Knows that in any state that he finds himself

Contentment with godliness suffices for him

For he's a vessel fitted to handle life's waves

As Destiny's own ordained to be the intrepid

That comes thru life's problems unscathed

Changes thru Drought (Cont'd)

The rains cease so ugly weeds can shrivel

So the good and lovely can be nourished

With little to distract and mislead in the way

Much can be afforded by grace through faith

So that the man who endures well in drought

Is well-prepared to abound in goodness in life

End

Earthly and Cosmic Clocks

There is a cosmic and an earthly clock to mind
With different purposes for each clock to govern
The earthly clock ticks as man searches for a path
For a way to reconnect with his divine root in time

The path of light is way that avails man an escape
From the leash and the ravages of earthly sojourn
Into the cosmic stream that entails the everlasting
Where death's cold hands can touch him no more

Such is a universal spirit freed of earthly shackles
To belong no more with the earth but the cosmos
For he is then under an interminable cosmic clock
Able to traverse in spirit 'tween heaven and earth

Earthly and Cosmic Clocks (Cont'd)

Many are stuck on earth with no hope of escape

And remain hopelessly lost in a dark endless loop

Not able to reconnect with their divine root in time

As objects lost because they rejected the true light

Quest to find that which was lost is life's true tale

Tis fate of the blind told in saga of the prodigal son

Man that finds his way home in allotted earthly time

Is one to be crowned with gifts that are everlasting

Earthly time for the race and the cosmic for a prize

Man's euphoric elation at the last-second shot made

And field goal kicked through to say the game is over

Are earthly events that hint to glory of timely escape

End

Better Fusion than Fission

The body that lacks grace is devoid of the spirit of Life
For such is the dead that prods along through fission
Where the parts devour each other much like cannibalism
In a frenzy of condemnable activities that so invites death

Though it may appear as a feast to the blind and unwary
Tis really the macabre dance of maggots in total delirium
Where the dying celebrate oblivious of impending doom
And neither peace nor fulfillment is afforded man's soul

The body filled with grace abounds with the spirit of Life
Such is alive and springs forth through a process of fusion
As parts reach out in cross pollination to create new life
Through an uplifting and joyful feasting in a spirit of love

Better Fusion than Fission (Cont'd)

Such do abound in the spirit of love, goodness and mercy

With truth and understanding there to sustain all within

As honey from each part fuse 'to sweet nectar of new life

With hand of God close to help and peace near to bless

Body that lacks grace is very evident for such cannot hide

He's the wise in his own eyes who loves not good counsel

And has difficulty in giving thanks or showing appreciation

Ever on the defensive and asks not for forgiveness easily

Such is a self-righteous knave blind to his many faults

With manipulative schemes aimed to win men's approval

A loud but false confessor of faith who does good deeds

Only when an audience is there to laud him with praise

Better Fusion than Fission (Cont'd)

He's purveyor and victim of the false that poses as real

Who's not able to perceive the spiritual from the earthly

The blind and oblivious who plods in a sea of darkness

In pride that invites death and keeps Life at a distance

End

From Land of Truth

The man that has journeyed to the distant land of truth
Has laid down his life to know in the stream of the pure
He has love for all people but despises the dark old ways
In the greater love he shows and greater truth he tells

The essence of the land far away is the good and perfect
The enduring availed in light of truth to sustain and fulfill
Such is entrusted to the traveler as love's precious gifts
So he can return to plant the good seed in willing hearts

Tis by journey of truth that darkened hearts are availed
A chance to catch a glimpse of the glorious and free
Glory that boasts not but is dignified in hushed splendor
And can lift up the eagle spirit that dares to kiss the sky

The Land of Truth (Cont'd)

Tis glory of the dew that covers all with life and hope

Same glory of the flower that smiles to welcome the sun

Ah! Such glory that man once knew and will know again

As that lost in the distant past is found again thru Truth

End

Power in Words

Anointed words and prescient knowledge
Used to address situations that life brings
So that the best outcome can always result
Is found thru the wisdom that God imparts

Words that change things for the better
And turn life's disappointments to blessings
To put back the spring in the sagging step
And restore vision to the flagging eyesight

Tis same that duly changes water into wine
Or that proverbial lemon into lemonade
And means for light to overcome darkness
So death's grip over mankind can be loosed

Power in Words (Cont'd)

Man bestowed with truth to reach all men

Can break the stony hearts with his words

Melt hardened minds with loving thoughts

And can find the pass thru life's mountains

He is one able to make the unbending yield

And can change things from the inside out

To reshape the lives flattened by the world

Into vessels of honor meet for God's use

End

Treasure the Soul

The man reborn in Light is the new Adam
Forewarned and prepared to thrive by faith
Such will have a temptress come into his life
To reprise Eve's role as catalyst in Eden's fall

The reborn lives by whispered divine truths
To take back his victory in light and love
He'll know his Achilles heel and be on guard
For to die once is the good payment required

The old self dies as man seeks after the true
So he can receive new life in God's anointing
The new is appointed to have honey delights
As divine glory borne from carcass of the old

Treasure the Soul (Cont'd)

To keep the treasure of the soul undefiled
Is not to fall for allures of the sweet and easy
For the tempter offers man sinful delights
Such pleasures that are but poison of the asp

To have compassion but not lose the soul
Is wisdom's counsel for all baptized in truth
For weight of judgment falls on the unwary
Those who know the truth and will not heed

The man that has been favored in judgment
Is a standard of reference to be used by God
And must treasure his soul above the earthy
For he's become a star to guide other seekers

End

Mirror of Indictment

Mankind is prone to reject the one justified
To be a standard of reference for judgment
For his way of living is a mirror of indictment
That brings injustice and wickedness to light

Mankind rather chooses the false and fake
A thief and robber in the ilk of Barabbas
Who regurgitates the old to take man back
To the dark past that should be forgotten

False one chosen and lauded by the people
Is a dark mirror that reflects not true light
He's the false chosen because he validates
The ways of transgression loved by the blind

Mirror of Indictment (Cont'd)

Sure tis convenient and less discomforting

When man is not confronted by his ugliness

But it is not expedient to set his spirit free

For to know not true self is to remain bound

He that knows not his true self will remain

A poisoned fountain and a damaged pillar

Who cannot withstand when faced by evil

And can ill-afford the enduring and precious

End

Heart of the True Confessor

True confession yields great power for man
Works to harmonize the two at war in him
To find elusive concord and common ground
Tween the old enemies of the spirit and flesh

The spirit that is free within man affords him
Divine peace that passes all understanding
The hidden truths will be revealed to such
As one fit to dine among an elect company

There is nothing new under the heavens
So declares the living and eternal truths
For all that'll ever be communicated to man
Has been inlaid as fine gold within creation

Heart of the True Confessor (Cont'd)

All is there for man to know when he is due
For the heart in which true confession exists
Where the flesh and the spirit fight no more
Has a sumptuous feast with Wisdom to attend

The heart without blemish is well informed
As one polished to reflect the divine mind
For such is a mirror framed in perfecting love
From which nothing can be hidden for long

The heart that is joined up with the divine
As the noble soul that lives by true confession
Will endure as Job and be dedicated as Noah
All in love that is as remorseful as David's

Heart of the True Confessor (Cont'd)

The true confessor intermeddles with Wisdom

From there to receive life's key of knowledge

Then is nothing new for man under the heaven

But all gold to be spied out and mined as needed

End

Higher and Greater

He that has received the gift of perception lives

According to a higher law and a greater purpose

Such is called to live in truth and light at all times

So that his spirit can remain ever ready to soar

Perception looks forward and never backwards

For the future gleams with the smile of renewal

But rear view of life often has tearful tales to tell

In sad echoes of the accusatory and recriminatory

Man that has the gift of perception is one set apart

Though misunderstood and vilified by blind masses

Yet he lives to serve humanity's cause in goodness

For he is certain that the future will vindicate him

Higher and Greater (Cont'd)

From place of goodwill and informed knowledge

The perceptive knows and speaks for welfare of all

As one rejected by many but embraced by the few

Who aspire for the greater and more fulfilling in life

End

The Climb

Many men answer the call to come up faith's summit
Such make valiant efforts but often end up on the ledge
A rest stop two-thirds of the way up in the long climb
That's a place of good hope but not heaven's table-land

Encumbered with issues of the flesh and worldly cares
Many reach the ledge to camp out and go no further
Such fall short of reaching the top for fear and doubt
For the prize sought for is not availed by will or bluster

There are a chosen few willing to let go of every thing
And count not the cost so they can make it to the top
Such are the ones bestowed with full divine anointing
The numbered who join the congregation at the summit

The Climb (Cont'd)

It takes a commitment and dedication to make the climb

Tis not for everyone but those called by the spirit of Love

Such that come to know the hidden truths and mysteries

Those chosen for everlasting habitation with the Father

End

Bond of Love

There's a bond of love that never gives up

A precious gift found only thru faithfulness

Tis unbreakable and can never be severed

Either in heaven above or on earth below

Tis bond of love that binds all saintly spirits

Who have already finished the good race

And leads them to seek the up and coming

And help such finish life's race in victory

Tis love that ascertains that the sojourner

Is neither stuck nor stranded in the way

When morn's about to bid night farewell

And the glorious prize is within good sight

Bond of Love (Cont'd)

The race for eternal life is through Love

Tis not about who finishes first or last

But about living to make sure that no one

Deserving is left behind or lost in the way

The saintly soul who's filled with wisdom

Empties himself for the brother without

While the one able to stand under mercy

Offers the legs to lift up the lame in grace

For the saintly the job is never finished

Until no one deserving is left on the way

For then is the good work well and done

All such ordained from foundation of time

End

Little Folly

Truth is the divine mirror by which each man

Comes to know and change the self for better

In it lies the power that can free man's spirit

To enable him soar to great and starry heights

Man asks to be told the truth but will not tell it

And so it becomes estranged as each day passes

For by mistruth and falsehood to varying degree

All men have come to follow as the world turns

Man knows that to tell lies is not the right thing

An acquired habit come about from Eden's fall

Sadly but yet he cannot desist from telling same

To eschew that which estranges the divine Spirit

Little Folly (Cont'd)

Tis like the drunkard with his innocent addiction

The seemingly little and recreational folly of life

Soon turns into a raging fire storm out of control

That burns him when and where he least expects

End

Seed of Bitterness

Man loses bits of himself with each lie he tells

Degrades himself and humanity as a whole

By telling lies he disrupts a divine connection

Distances himself from the heavenly Father

The man that cannot cease from telling lies

Is infected with an evil virus in the core within

He's given way for a harmful species to invade

And to take over the landscape of his mind

Man tells lies in order to gain undue advantage

Either in the material or other worldly ways

But to tell lies sits not right in the human psyche

And most look for justification in order to tell it

Seed of Bitterness (Cont'd)

To live by hook or crook and any other means

Where man lives only on a risk and reward basis

And others matter little if one can have his way

Is a sad irony of the short lived and regrettable

For lies plant seeds of bitterness among men

And leave a dark patch lodged in their souls

But truth is the bitter but wholesome medicine

That soothes all souls and brings needed healing

End

Morning Appointed for Truth

The hidden truths are not understood in one helping
But are progressively revealed in the passage of time
Greater light of understanding comes to bear in his life
As the believer grows and matures in the inner man

There are some truths that can never be understood
Until the season divinely appointed for them arrives
There are like seeds that remain in prolonged burial
In the good fertilized soil until the dew of heaven falls

There is a morning appointed for each hidden truth
That has to dawn before its fullness can be understood
But with mankind in the last days of this far gone age
Much has been availed for the true seeker to find

Morning Appointed for Truth (Cont'd)

God has bestowed the faithful with due knowledge

Of the hidden which constitute the meat of the word

Such is for only the matured in light to comprehend

As keys to help man understand the mystifying in life

End

From Same Womb

The Father's glory reflects on all that he draws near

Though he remains unseen with the eyes of men

For close to his heart is the place without darkness

Where all who come into are commended 'to light

Those born-again are conformed by love and truth

To stumble no longer but walk in fullness of light

In a stream of righteousness evoked from above

And divine touch that adds light to their endeavors

Such are like points of light in a world of darkness

Embalmed in truth within that covers them without

Same it is that sanctifies and protects man from evil

From wickedness that seeks to mar all things good

From Same Womb (Cont'd)

All who come to the place close to the Father's heart

Will have the divine magnetism duly induced in them

Tis the touch of Midas that purifies the base into gold

Magnetism that turns sinful men into vessels of glory

There is a magnetism when truth is imparted in love

To draw men to the Father and source of all goodness

Tis impulse that is the gain of belief and loss of doubt

A precious gift that affirms the bond of Love with Life

Tis impulse that leads back to the home once known

For all who come to know the Father and his sons

Were once known by them and are spiritual kindred

Vessels of same mold come forth out of same womb

End

Good and Lovely

The faithful is called to hope for the best in life
The uplifting that is lovely and of good report
And to share words of truth with the blinded
Where the world's noise has beclouded true light

The noise of the world dims and dampens souls
Fills men's mind with much unbecoming thoughts
Which takes shape to drag down lives in dust
For tis his thoughts that become reality for man

The mind that is not cluttered with much wants
Leaves enough room for the important to thrive
For such is cleared of undesirable debris of life
And freed from the cloudiness that inhibits vision

Good and Lovely (Cont'd)

Clarity comes when cloudiness has been cleared

For with good vision much can be clearly seen

So the nature and state of things can be known

And room made for the good and lovely to thrive

The good and lovely count with the precious in life

In a treasure-chest to be held very near and dear

But the bad and undesirable have to be discarded

Into a dust-bin that must be kept far and distant

End

OTHER BOOKS BY KALU ONWUKA INCLUDE-

(Poetry)

Anthems in the Glorious Dawn

In Enchantment of Eternity

Tones of the Stellar

A Splendid Awakening

(Studies for Spirit, Mind and Body)

Nuggets of Resurrection

Pulses of the Divine Heart

Etching for the Faithful Heart

No Hurry to Horeb

(Quotations and Insights)

Capsules of Divine Splendor

All titles are available for purchase through Granada Publishers at **granadapublishing.com**. The author can be contacted through his website at **kaluonwuka.com**.

Kalu Onwuka is a prolific author who writes about faith walk in this new age of man's spiritual awareness. His books offer tit-bits on how to find a balance between the earthly and heavenly. He is a man of many accomplishments and draws his inspirational insights from many areas of life's experiences. The perceptive reader will find his books to be quite interesting and very enriching. He is a *Teacher, Poet, Lyricist, Electrical Engineer and Entrepreneur.* He lives with his wife in Southern California and they have five children

He is the author of the *On the Golden Strand* series which are discourses that encapsulate his spiritual experiences on the journey of spiritual transformation. These include *The Nuggets of Resurrection, Pulses of the Divine Heart, Etching for the Faithful Heart, No Hurry to Horeb* and other books in the work. He is also the author of the *Poems in Faithfulness to the Divine* Series which are books of poetry and songs. These include *Anthems in the Glorious Dawn, In Enchantment of Eternity, Tones of the Stellar, The Melody of Light, Capsules of Divine Splendor*, and other books on the way.

www.ingramcontent.com/pod-product-compliance
Lightning Source LLC
Chambersburg PA
CBHW060152050426
42446CB00013B/2778